MW00640444

What Every Girl Should Know…

About boys and relationships

Mia Carroll

Copyright © 2012 by Mia Carroll

All rights reserved. No part of this book may be reproduced,
scanned or distributed in any printed or electronic form without
permission, except for brief quotations in critical reviews or
articles.

For information: mmiacarroll@gmail.com

ISBN-10: 0615777570
ISBN-13: 978-0615777573

INTRODUCTION

A long time ago, well maybe not that long, I made the decision not to have children. This is something I chose for very personal reasons and I'm fine with it.

However, I am an aunt to five young girls that are going to start dating soon and have no idea what's in store for them and their romantic futures.

This book was written as a gift to those five girls, and any other girl out there who could use a little advice; whether they are already dating or before they start experiencing their own great adventures and love affairs.

This does not mean that I am a relationship expert, but, I must admit I have had my fair share of romances.

The suggestions in this book are my personal opinion. Some I feel are common sense, others I've experienced. You may not agree with all of them and I'm sure you could probably add some of your own.

With any luck, this little book could prevent a broken heart or two. At the very least, I hope it puts a smile on your face.

DEDICATION

For Isabella, Anna, Alessandra, Emma and Elisa.

May this book give you guidance when you need it,
help when you want it and hopefully make things a
little easier.

-1-

Don't chase boys. They
will come to you.

-2-

Chivalry is never
outdated.

-3-

Sex is overrated.

-4-

Do not rush into things.
Ever.

-5-

If a guy doesn't treat you how you want when you're dating, he will certainly not do it when you're married.

-6-

Under no circumstances make a sex tape. No. Matter. What.

-7-

Drunken women are not attractive.

-8-

Slutty girls may get attention but it's not the good kind.

-9-

Bad boys are attractive but good boys are keepers.

-10-

Age does matter.

-11-

Size matters. It shouldn't, but it does.

-12-

Respect yourself.

-13-
Nobody knows what your relationship is really like except the two of you.

-14-

Do not date your friend's exes.

-15-

Don't date your ex's friends.

-16-

Never date your relatives exes.

-17-

Do not cheat.

-18-
Allow yourself a couple of days to mourn your ended relationship then get on with your life.

-19-
Don't jump from boy to boy.

-20-
Allow a reasonable amount of time between relationships. At least three months.

-21-
Never ever take nude pictures. EVER.

-22-
Do not beg for attention. Or anything else for that matter.

-23-

If your mother doesn't like him from the get go, trust her instincts. She knows.

-24-

If your pet doesn't like him from the get go, end it immediately! They know best.

-25-

No sex on the first date.

-26-

No fondling of any kind
on the first date either.

-27-

If he doesn't like
animals, he's not for you.
That simple.

-28-

Sometimes, things are
not all about you.

-29-

If you call and he doesn't answer, leave a message if need be and be done with it. Do not keep calling non-stop.

-30-

Do not drunk dial your ex. That never ends well.

-31-

Be very careful what you post online.

-32-

Be as discreet and private as possible.

-33-

Try not to criticize.

-34-

Learn how to make his favorite dessert.

-35-

Nobody dies from a broken heart. No matter how much you may want to.

-36-

Not every guy you like is going to like you back. It's no big deal.

-37-
You are absolutely beautiful. Never let a guy make you feel differently.

-38-
If a guy says he's going
to call and doesn't, he's
not worth your time.

-39-
If a guy takes too long to
call, he's not worth your
time either.

-40-
Sometimes a guy truly is
just not that into you.
His loss.

-41-

Follow your instincts. If something doesn't feel right, it most likely isn't.

-42-

Jealousy is never good. It can ruin a relationship.

-43-

Don't stay with someone out of fear of being alone.

-44-

Do not send out mixed signals. If you don't like him, act like it.

-45-

Being with someone
for money is never
right. If at some point
in your life you decide
to go that way be
prepared to put up
with A LOT.

-46-

There's most definitely plenty of fish in the sea. That saying is very true.

-47-

If a guy pushes you to do something you don't want to, run for the hills.

-48-

No means no. ALWAYS.

-49-

Give yourself plenty of
time to get over your
ex before you even
consider being friends.
You'll regret it if you
don't.

-50-

Do not use tears to get your way.

-51-

Do not use sex to get your way.

-52-

Do not threaten to end things on a whim. It just might happen.

-53-
Always mean what you
say.

-54-
Do not let someone
emotionally blackmail
you.

-55-
Do not cheat on
someone so they will
break up with you.

-56-

Be **absolutely** sure that you are ready to hear the truth when you ask for it.

-57-

Be sure you both want
the same things before
you get too serious.

-58-

If you are both not
heading towards the
same goals end the
relationship. You're just
delaying the inevitable.

-59-

Everybody has baggage.

-60-

Never, ever, under any circumstances, have unprotected sex.

-61-

Do not stay with someone out of pity or because you don't want to hurt their feelings.

-62-

Do not pick a fight at 11pm on a weeknight.

-63-

Don't try to make someone jealous. It's not worth it and could come back to bite you in the ass.

-64-

If something is bothering you, talk about it. Don't say "nothing" when he asks you what's wrong.

-65-

If you are having a disagreement, do not drag a topic on and on. Say what you need to and leave it at that.

-66-

Do <u>not</u> bring up past mistakes every time you have an argument. That's over and done with. Otherwise, end the relationship.

-67-
Friends with benefits never work out.

-68-
Jealous ex-girlfriends are not your problem, they are his.

-69-
Guys will never think the same way you do. Don't expect them to.

-70-

Don't be too available.

-71-

When you've made a mistake apologize and mean it.

-72-

Don't give up your life and friends for any guy. Have your own thing going on.

-73-

Let him have his own thing as well, no suffocating.

-74-

Do not make him the center of your universe.

-75-

Be hard to get.

-76-

Always be upfront.

-77-

Don't fawn over the good looking ones.

-78-

Be sure he makes you laugh.

-79-

Be very sure he doesn't make you cry.

-80-
If someone cheats on
you, don't dwell,
obsess or go crazy.
Rise above it and move
on. I know it's hard
but you're better than
that.

-81-

If you decide to forgive an infidelity, be sure to honestly forgive it. If you can't do this, end the relationship.

-82-

Always be grateful for admirers. Even if you don't feel the same way.

-83-
Avoid making a scene in public. Your business is only your business; no one else's.

-84-

Don't trust a guy who
doesn't want you to meet
his friends or his parents.

-85-

Travel at least once
(preferably out of the
country) with your
boyfriend. It will tell you
a lot about your
relationship.

-86-

If you don't want your parents to meet him, he's not the guy for you.

-87-

Many men have very fragile egos. Keep that in mind.

-88-

If he doesn't say it, don't assume it.

-89-

Men tell you exactly who they are from the beginning. Keep your eyes and ears wide open.

-90-

If he's too into himself,
he won't be into you.

-91-

If he never has time for
you, cut him loose.

-92-

Guys are not your
responsibility. Do not try
to fix or save them.

-93-

Do not try to change him, he is who he is. Love him like that or not at all.

-94-

Same thing goes for you; if he tries to change you he's not the one.

-95-

Give him time to miss you.

-96-

Do not get involved with a guy you work with. That never ends well.

-97-

If he cheats with you, he'll cheat on you. Truer words have never been spoken.

-98-

Excessive PDA is not cute.

-99-

If you like someone else, be brave and end things.

-100-

Break up in person. It's hard but it's the right thing to do.

-101-

Guys aren't mind readers. Speak up.

-102-
Don't expect him to do
something just because
it's what you would do.
Not. Gonna. Happen.

-103-

Don't nag. It doesn't suit you.

-104-

Don't whine either.

-105-

Baby talk has a time and place. Probably an age limit too.

-106-

Do not criticize his mother.

-107-

Don't tell a guy he reminds you of your father.

-108-

Drugs are NOT cool. Neither are the guys that do them. Don't waste your time.

-109-

If he stops calling, don't overanalyze things. He just did. Move on.

-110-

Don't demand that he call or see you. If he wants to, he will.

-111-

Do demand respect and consideration. If you don't get these, end things immediately.

-112-

Don't let him take you for granted.

-113-
Don't take him for granted.

-114-
Compromise.

-115-
Don't be a victim to your hormones.

-116-
Pick your battles.

-117-
Don't fight over a boy, especially with a friend.

-118-
Don't pretend to like something just for a boy.

-119-
Be genuine.

-120-
Sweet does not mean pushover.

-121-

He's not going to change just because you love him so much.

-122-

If he doesn't want you to spend time with your family, he's bad news.

-123-

If you don't even want to introduce him to your family, he's even worse news.

-124-

If he loves you he will wait. This applies to <u>everything</u>.

-125-
Never underestimate the power of a home cooked meal.

-126-
Let him do the dishes.

-127-
A guy needs to know how to pack his own suitcase or else you'll be doing it for the rest of his life.

-128-

Always be polite to his family. You never know, they might be your family one day.

-129-

Ask what to bring when they invite you to dinner. If they say nothing, bring something anyway. Even if it's just flowers.

-130-

If a guy messes up, you are allowed to give him a second chance if you really want to. **<u>ONE</u>**.

-131-

If you say it's over, then it's over. Don't back down.

-132-

People change, relationships change. It's all part of life. Go with the flow.

-133-

Don't be too hard on the rebound guys.

-134-
Never settle.

-135-
Bake him cookies for no reason.

-136-
Cut him some slack if he forgets an anniversary. It happens to the best of us.

-137-
Know what you want,
but more importantly,
know what you don't
want.

WHAT EVERY GIRL SHOULD KNOW

-138-
Make out in the rain.

-139-
Disney is not real life.

-140-
Unfortunately neither is
Jane Austen.

-141-
But do hold out for your
Mr. Darcy. He's out
there.

58

-142-

Do not obsess over the other girls. You are the prettiest. Period.

-143-

Most men are threatened by strong, independent women. That's their problem, not yours.

-144-

Shoes say a lot about a guy.

-145-

You have to be attracted to him or else it's not going to work out.

-146-

All relationships have ups and downs. If there are more downs than ups, it's time to move on.

-147-

Look into their family's medical history before you decide to have children with someone.

-148-

Self-confidence is the best makeup.

-149-

Smelling good makes everyone more attractive.

-150-

Beware of talkers, they're usually not doers.

-151-

If he doesn't do it, don't expect it.

-152-

Once the trust is gone, the relationship is over.

-153-
Thinking about something does not automatically make it so.

-154-
If a guy says he needs time to think and figure things out, it's time to move on.

-155-
Time heals pretty much everything.

-156-
If you're not ready to break up, don't complain about him to your friends and family. They might not forgive and forget.

-157-

Don't reject someone for fear of being rejected.

-158-

Your first love isn't always your true love.

-159-

I hate to say this but when your mother says you're too young to have a serious boyfriend, she's right.

-160-
Take very good care of your reputation, it will precede you.

-161-
Sometimes the timing is just off.

-162-
Avoid drama. Nothing good comes from it.

-163-
Some people move on faster than others.

-164-

It is very easy for guys to call a girl crazy. Don't give them any reason to.

-165-

Beware of men that throw the L word around too easily and too early in the relationship.

-166-

Every relationship is different. No comparing.

-167-
There are things you simply will never understand about the opposite sex. Don't drive yourself crazy trying to.

-168-

Allow yourself to be
loved.

-169-

NEVER get involved
with a married man.
Pretty obvious, but it
seems some people need
a reminder.

-170-

Good hygiene is
extremely important.

-171-
So are good manners.

-172-
Learn proper etiquette, you never know when you will be dining with a prince.

-173-
Motels are no place for ladies.

-174-

Set your limits from the very beginning.

-175-

If you're questioning whether you should break up or not, you probably should.

-176-

Learn from the bad ones so you can identify the good ones.

-177-

Most of the time guys really are thinking about "nothing".

-178-

Refrain from bashing his friends.

-179-

You do not need to see or talk to your ex in order to get closure.

-180-
If a friend steals your boyfriend, be grateful. She helped you get rid of a bad boyfriend and an even worse friend.

-181-
Enjoy being alone, it's
one of the greatest
things.

-182-
Wit is extremely alluring.

-183-
Wisecracks not so much.
Learn to tell the
difference.

-184-
Gentlemen have no
memory, as do ladies.

-185-
The truth ALWAYS
comes out at one point
or another. Be the first
to tell it.

-186-
Sometimes, the idea of
love is better than the
actual thing.

-187-
When in a relationship give it your all. If things don't work out you will know it was not because you didn't try hard enough.

-188-

If he compares you to his past girlfriends, he's got to go.

-189-

Before the age of 25 guys usually do want one thing only. Choose wisely.

-190-

Past relationship disasters are not first date conversation topics.

-191-

Don't trust anyone from the get go, give them time to prove themselves first.

-192-

Infatuation is not the same as love, don't mix those up.

-193-

Neither is sex. Get that straight.

-194-
Nobody likes being
blown off. Be nice.

-195-
If one of your goals is to
get married, give your
relationship a time limit;
don't let it drag on for
years on end.

-196-
One night stands are
forbidden.

-197-
Don't embarrass him in front of his friends.

-198-
Take care of him when he's sick. Within reason of course.

-199-
It's not good to have too many expectations. You could be disappointed.

-200-

Don't put anyone up on a pedestal.

-201-

It's all in the attitude.

-202-

Don't boss guys around.

-203-

If he doesn't know you exist, you shouldn't know he exists either.

-204-
Guys will always want you the minute they can't have you.

-205-
What goes around does
indeed come around.
Don't forget.

-206-
Time apart is good for
the soul and a
relationship.

-207-
Never do something just
so a guy likes you.

-208-

Never alter your body just because a guy wants you to.

-209-

You do not own anyone and you are not property. Everyone is free to do as they wish.

-210-

Don't say things just to provoke him.

-211-

If he really likes you he will like you no matter the length of your hair, the state of your complexion or your bra size.

-212-
Sometimes, the best thing you can do is step back and take some time to breathe.

-213-
No stalking. That's just beneath you.

-214-
There comes a point in life when playing games is just a waste of time.

-215-

Let the guy make the
first move.

-216-

On again off again
relationships are a waste
of your time. Avoid
them at all costs.

-217-

Fall for a guy because of
what he does and not
what he says.

-218-
Guys should open doors.
No matter what century
we're in.

-219-
If a guy messes up in the
first two weeks, walk
away. Trust me, you may
be saving yourself years
of suffering.

-220-
Elude situations where a guy might expect more than you are willing to give.

-221-
There are times when you have to break up, no matter how much you love someone. It hurts, a lot. You'll survive.

-222-
You do not need a boyfriend in order to be happy.

39640553R00055

Made in the USA
Middletown, DE
18 March 2019